WHERE ARE MY MONSTERS?

i had FOURTEEN MONSTERS, now i have none. . .

i LEFT THE WiNDOW OPEN, NOW THEY'VE ALL GONE !

FORGIVE ME FOR SUCH A SILLY
BLUNDER....

WHERE COULD THEY BE
I WONDER...?

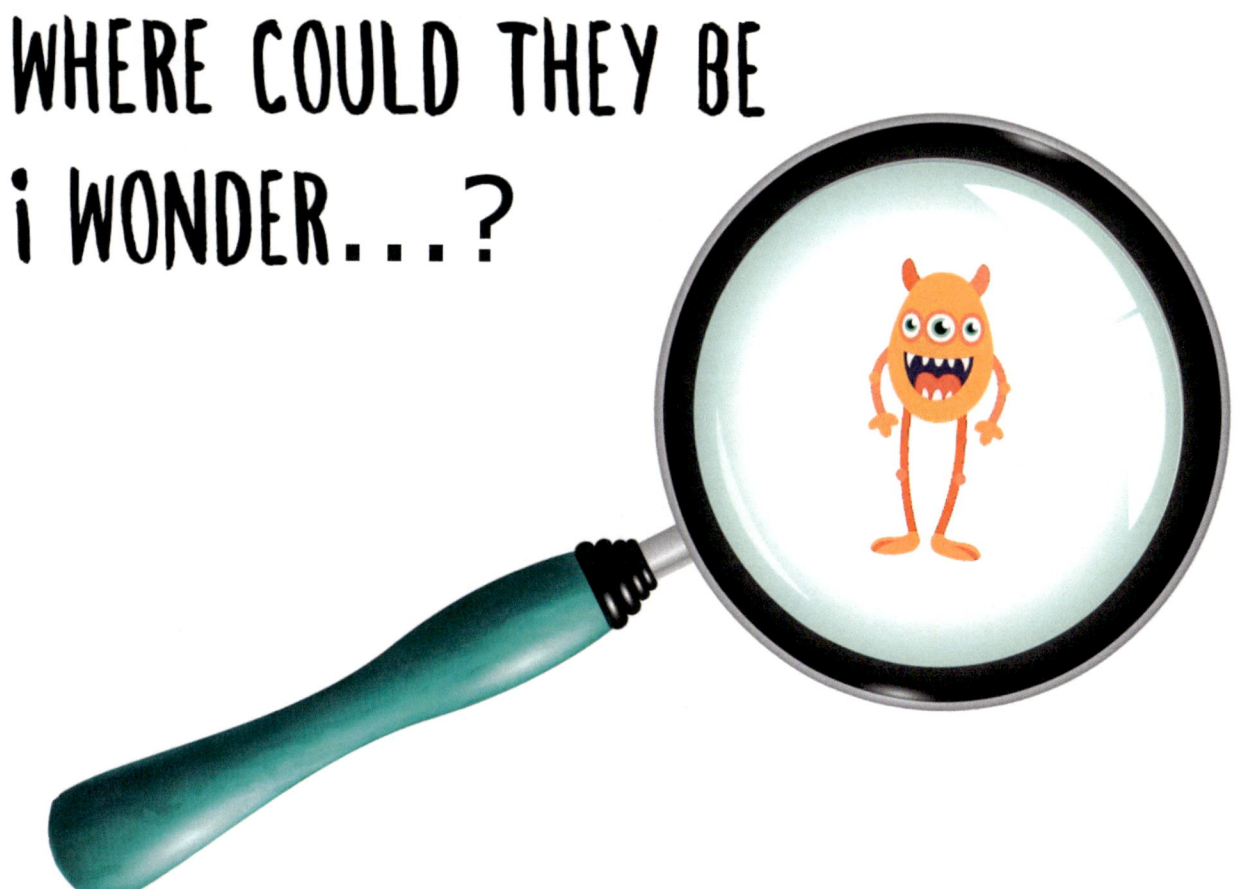

HE'S RUNNING WILD
AND FREE.
PLEASE HELP ME FIND

TIMBURLY

He's not a cat.
He's also not a dog.

Can you spot

BABBLEBOG?

WHERE'S

WOMPUS

GOT TO?
Can you help me, because i
haven't got a clue.

This is
Nitti

i think she's lost in the big city.

CAN YOU SPOT GERMY?

HE'S BEEN ON QUITE THE JOURNEY.

Restaurant

i've lost

MiLLOY

SHE'S A GiRL, NOT A BOY.

SPABBLE LIKES TO HAVE FUN. HE'S GOT A SPOTTY GREEN BODY AND A BRIGHT RED TONGUE!

THANK YOU FOR HELPING, YOU'RE EVER SO KIND.

SEVEN MONSTERS FOUND, SEVEN LEFT TO FIND...

He's the same size as a poodle. Have you seen Kadoodle?

HELP ME FIND

GOOB

iF YOU WiLL.
HE'S GOT AN UNCLE NAMED PETRA
AND AN AUNTiE CALLED PHiL.

Can you find

McDiddle?

He doesn't like standing in the middle.

SHE'S VERY RARE.
HAVE YOU SEEN
EGGLES
ANYWHERE?

Can you find
GRUMP
for me?
He needs to come home for his tea.

i KNOW SHE MUST BE AROUND.
SO iS

FLONKY

ANYWHERE TO BE FOUND?

i love my
WiNKYBOO
but where has she got to?

THANK YOU!

MY MONSTERS ARE FOUND!

NOW THEY'RE COMING BACK HOME, ALL SAFE AND SOUND.

THE END!

ALSO AVAILABLE:

FIND THE SILLY ANIMALS!

In this fun picture puzzle book, you'll travel through forests, deserts, farms, a pirate ship and many more locations, searching for some really silly animals. See if you can find the Tiger-Tortoise and the Monkey-Pig - and don't forget the Elephant-Shark along the way!

ALSO AVAILABLE:

WHERE'S THE POO?

In this fun, spot the poo puzzle game, you'll travel through schools, car parks, a sunny beach, an alien planet, a winter wonderland and many more locations in the search for those pesky poops. See if you can find Poobert, Mrs Poopington and Ploppy Doo- and don't forget Stinky along the way!

Made in the USA
San Bernardino, CA
11 February 2018